Revised Edition

Transformed Into His Likeness

A Handbook for Putting Off Sin and Putting On Righteousness

by

Armand P. Tiffe

Copyright, 2005, 2018 by Focus Publishing
PO Box 665
Bemidji, Minnesota 56619
All Rights Reserved

ISBN: 1-885904-52-5
Cover Photo by Glenn Ferguson
Cover & Book Design by Michelle Hanevold

PRINTED IN THE UNITED STATES OF AMERICA

This book is affectionately dedicated to my wife, Kathy. Honey, you are truly a Proverbs 31 wife and mother.

Transformed Into His Likeness
A Handbook for Putting Off Sin and Putting On Righteousness

Revised Edition

by
Armand P. Tiffe

This book emphasizes growth in Christ-likeness. It is a workbook to help you be what God wants you to be. The introductory teaching is a clear, concise, easy-to-understand explanation of how a believer changes sinful habits and tendencies.

The "Put Off - Put On" List is very useful in identifying common problems with which many Christians struggle, and provides biblical solutions to those problems. One of the exclusive features of this "List" is that many of the topics are not found in a Bible Concordance.

The "Put Off - Put On" List is categorized into several areas. The first 69 deal with a broad range of personal issues; numbers 70-85 deal with worldly-mindedness; 86-97 list hindrances to spiritual growth; 98-103 are unique to husbands and fathers; 104-109 are unique to wives and mothers, and 110-114 are unique to teens and children.

The Personal Transformation Worksheet at the back is designed to help a person implement into everyday life the change that God desires. An explanation of the worksheet and an example of how to work through it are also provided.

A Note on the Scripture References: Common practice is to list references in the chronological order of the Bible, and for most topics that is how they appear in this book. However, for some topics they are out of sequence so as to start with the most pertinent Scripture for that particular topic, or for the purpose of developing a greater impact on the reader.

The strength of this resource is that it is a complete package. It explains the biblical process of change, helps identify where personal change is needed, provides pertinent Scripture references to problem areas, and offers a practical worksheet to walk you through the change process and help you implement biblical change into your life. May God use this resource as a tool to transform you into the likeness of His Son!

A Word to Counselors and Disciple Makers:
This is a helpful resource to use with those you are counseling or discipling. Homework may be assigned by you for the person to work through in areas of need. A suggested procedure for using this resource in a counseling and discipleship ministry is provided at the end of the book.

All Scripture is breathed out by God and profitable for teaching, for reproof, for correction, and for training in righteousness, that the man of God may be competent, equipped for every good work.

2 Timothy 3:16-17

*"Do not be conformed to this world, **but be transformed** by the renewal of your mind..."* (Romans 12:2, emphasis mine). Transformation is personal change that begins within. It is complete change from the inside out as the Spirit of God is at work transforming your way of thinking, speaking, and behaving. However, for personal change to take place in your life, you must have the proper mindset.

The Proper Mindset

Change is necessary in a Christian's life. The Lord never intends for any of His children to remain as they are, but to grow in Christ-likeness. The normal course of a Christian's life involves growth in Christ-like character qualities. (In fact, this is how we experience the abundant life Jesus speaks of in John 10:10). Spiritual growth is a lifelong process that begins at conversion. The Holy Spirit will lead you and empower you in this process of change, but you must do your part. God has designed the transformation process to be a cooperative venture between His Spirit and you. Romans 8:13 expresses this cooperative venture: *"if **by the Spirit you** put to death the deeds of the body, you will live"* (emphasis mine). Notice that it is *"by the Spirit"* that you are able to put to death the misdeeds of the flesh. But, it also says that *"you"* must do it. It is not the Holy Spirit who is commanded to put to death the deeds of the flesh, but the believer. However, this is not to be done in your own power, but through the power of the Spirit who indwells you as you exercise faith and obedience. God and the believer each have a role to play in the transformation process. It must be *"by the Spirit"* and His power, but *"you put to death"* shows that a believer must also take an active role in overcoming his or her particular sinful tendencies. (See also, Galatians 2:20; Philippians 2:12-13).

The Liberating Truth

The proper mindset includes an understanding of the nature of your union and identity in Christ. The liberating truth, according to Romans Chapter 6, is that sin's power over you has been broken. At conversion, through faith in the sacrificial and substitutionary work of Christ on the cross, God has delivered you from the ruling power of sin. The glorious truth of Romans 6 is that you *"died to sin"* (v. 2)... you have been *"set free from sin"* (v. 7, 18)... so that you *"might walk in newness of life"* (v. 4). In other words, by virtue of your union with Christ, you have a new status that radically alters your relationship to sin. By God's grace, you have been set free from the bondage of sin; free to overcome sinful habits, thoughts, and tendencies; free to live for Christ. You can now choose not to obey the temptations and enticements to sin. We are exhorted in verse 11, *"So you also must consider yourselves dead to sin and alive to God in Christ Jesus."* You must grasp and believe this liberating work of Christ in your life in order to live in the reality of who you are in Christ. Verse 14 declares, *"For sin will have no dominion over you."* You can now live a life of righteousness! Sin is no longer your master, reigning over you, as it did before your new life in Christ. This is the result of your spiritual union with Christ. The glorious truth is that His atoning death for sin became your death to sin. His burial became the burial to your old sinful life. His resurrection to life became your resurrection to a new life. This is your new spiritual position in Christ! As a result, this means that you now have the potential in Christ to live a new godly life (see Romans 6:1-14). Personal change begins with the proper mindset. Then you must understand how change is experienced in everyday life. [A more detailed explanation of a believer's union and identity in Christ is available by the author titled, "The Liberating Truth of Romans 6" through Focus Publishing. It is an eye-opener and faith-builder for any struggling Christian].

The Biblical Process Of Change

One reason why many Christians fail to change is because they try to change by merely breaking bad habits and suppressing bad thoughts. Many Christians hold to what can be called a "religion of avoidance." What I mean by this is that they put forth an effort into trying to stop thinking about something or stop doing something they know is wrong and harmful to their walk with the Lord. However, true and lasting change will not take place in your life if you only concentrate on trying to stop something you know is wrong. **A key biblical principle for personal change can be simply stated as follows: We don't merely break bad habits or suppress bad thoughts, we replace them.** This is called "The Principle of Replacement." It is a principle that runs throughout Scripture. The Bible does not merely tell us to stop ungodly behavioral practices and ways of thinking, but to *replace* them with godly behavioral practices and ways of thinking. Basically, the process of change is described in the Bible by three key terms: **PUT OFF – RENEW – PUT ON.** You are to **Put Off** your old sinful way of life, renew your mind with the truths of Scripture, and **Put On** the new godly way of life. Ephesians 4:22-24 clearly describes this process:

*22 To **Put Off** your old self, which belongs to your former manner of life and is corrupt through deceitful desires, 23 and to be **Renewed** in the spirit of your minds, 24 and to **Put On** the new self, created after the likeness of God in true righteousness and holiness (emphasis mine; cf. Colossians 3:1-10).*

The "Put Off – Put On" Dynamic

Ephesians 4:22 says you are to "*Put Off* your old self." The "old self" is who you were before your conversion; the old you with your old way of thinking, speaking, and behaving. You are to identify habitual patterns, practices, and tendencies that are not God-honoring, and cast them off, like dirty clothes. Habit patterns, practices, and tendencies refer to sins that you are characterized by, not an occasional problem.

The Holy Spirit will use God's Word to convict you of sin (2 Timothy 3:16-17; 4:2; Titus 1:9; Hebrews 4:12). He may also use a counselor, friend, or your spouse to reveal blind spots in your life. As these sins are brought to your attention, you must confess them, acknowledging your sin against God and others (James 5:16; 1 John 1:8-9).

However, the process of change is not complete by simply telling God or others that you are sorry, or by asking Him or others to forgive you. For example, it is not enough for a habitual liar to tell God he is sorry every time he lies. He is only acknowledging that he has sinned. For true change to take place, he must now become a habitual truth teller (see Ephesians 4:25). It is not enough to Put Off the old self; you must also "Put On the new self" for true and lasting change to take place also (Ephesians 4:24). The "new self" refers to the new godly way of life; how God wants you to think, speak, and behave. You must not only take off the old dirty clothes, you must also Put On the new clean clothes. It is not enough to Put Off the old ways if they are not replaced with biblical alternatives. The old self is put off by establishing the new self. This is the key to personal change. The Christian life is not just about eliminating sin; it is about growing in righteousness. In fact, this is how we obtain true peace and joy — by pursuing righteousness, not just in avoiding sin.

Remember the principle of replacement. God intends for you to pursue the **Putting On** of the biblical alternatives to whatever sin you are trying to **Put Off**. Merely trying to concentrate on stopping a bad habit or thought is much more difficult. Concentrating on what needs to be **Put On** will be very helpful in overcoming sinful tendencies that you have practiced for years (Philippians 3:12-14; 4:8). These sinful habitual patterns are learned ways of living. We reinforce their hold over us and become characterized by them through repetition and practice. Therefore, we can weaken their grip on our lives as new godly ways of living are learned through daily practice. We are exhorted in 1 Timothy 4:7, "*Train yourself for godliness.*" (See also, Hebrews 5:14; 1 Timothy 4:7, "*Train yourself for godliness.*")

Philippians 4:11; 1 Corinthians 6:9-11; Romans 6:16-17). Change is a gradual process that takes place as you are enabled by the Spirit of God to put into practice biblical principles for living. As you do this over time, new ways of living will take shape, and you will be transformed.

Inner Renewal: Getting to the Heart of Behavior

Personal transformation is more than merely modifying external behavior. We are to become more like Christ from the inside out. In Ephesians 4:23, you will notice that in between the kind of person you are to put off and put on are the words, "*and to be* **Renewed** *in the spirit of your minds*" (emphasis mine). This speaks of an inner renewal. The "*spirit*" of your mind is the inner person — the core of your being — what the Bible most often refers to as the *heart*. The heart is the source of our thoughts and desires. It is essential to understand that everything we say and do is initiated and motivated by the thoughts and desires of our heart. Notice the importance the Bible places on the heart in Proverbs 4:23: "*Keep your heart with all vigilance, for from it flow the springs of life.*" This verse alerts us to an important priority: "*Keep your heart,*" i.e., guard it against ungodly influences and worldly ways of thinking; and do it "*with all vigilance*" because "*from it flow the springs of life.*" Everything we do in word and deed flows from the thoughts and desires of the heart. Observe what the Bible says about this.

> *For out of the abundance of the heart the mouth speaks. The good person out of his good treasure brings forth good, and the evil person out of his evil treasure brings forth evil (Matthew 12:34-35).*

> *For from within, out of the heart of man, come evil thoughts, sexual immorality, theft, murder, adultery, coveting, wickedness, deceit, sensuality, envy, slander, pride, foolishness. All these evil things come from within, and they defile a person (Mark 7:21-23).*

> *What causes quarrels and what causes fights among you? Is it not this, that your passions are at war within you? You desire and do not have, so you murder. You covet and cannot obtain, so you fight and quarrel (James 4:1-2).*

Notice that these Scriptures teach that sin begins in the heart and expresses itself outwardly in our words and behavior. Therefore, change in behavior begins with a change in the heart. The put off—put on process includes sins of the heart. You must go to the root of the problem in order to change bad fruit. The thoughts and desires that occupy your heart will influence your words and behavior. For real change to take place, you must look beyond external behavior and ask yourself, "What thought or desire is occupying my heart right now that is influencing my words, actions, and behavior?" Pray that God will expose any selfish desires, unbiblical beliefs, and worldly ways of thinking that are hindering your walk with Him, hurting your closest relationships, and undermining your peace and joy in Christ. King David understood this when he prayed, "*Search me, O God, and know my heart! Try me and know my thoughts! And see if there be any grievous way in me, and lead me in the way everlasting!*" (Psalm 139:23-24; cf. Hebrews 4:12-13).

God knows that you cannot live out the Christian life unless you are being renewed in your inner being (Ephesians 3:16). You must realize that over the years you have developed sinful tendencies and inclinations. When you placed faith in Christ He forgave you, cleansed you of your sin, and broke sin's power over you (Romans 6:6). However, you still find that your old tendencies are not totally gone and they continue to draw you into sin. That is why you must be renewed in the spirit of your mind.

How Does Inner Renewal Take Place?

The primary means the Spirit of God uses is His Word, The Bible. In John 17:17, Jesus prays to the Father on behalf of His disciples, "Sanctify them in the truth; your word is truth." We renew our bodies by taking in good food, and likewise, we renew our minds by taking in the Word of God. Inner renewal is a process that takes place when we think in new biblical ways as we read, study, and meditate on the truths of Scripture.

How can a young man keep his way pure? By guarding it according to your word.... I have stored up your word in my heart, that I might not sin against you.... Your word is a lamp to my feet and a light to my path (Psalm 119:9, 11, 105).

If you abide in my word, you are truly my disciples, and you will know the truth, and the truth will set you free (John 8:31-32).

All Scripture is breathed out by God and profitable for teaching, for reproof, for correction, and for training in righteousness, that the man of God may be competent, equipped for every good work (2 Timothy 3:16-17).

Personal transformation is the process by which the *Spirit of God* uses the *Word of God* and changes us to become like the *Son of God*. This is a lifelong process. You are being renewed by God's work of illumination in your heart when truth enlightens it. You are being renewed as you are continually grasping and appropriating the truths of God's Word. You are being renewed when your thoughts and desires are becoming more and more Christ-like. Each time you choose to replace a sinful thought and desire to a more biblical one, you are being renewed. This inner renewal will lead to **Putting Off** your old way of life and **Putting On** a new way of life that is pleasing to God.

This is a process that takes time and the exercise of your will in the power of the Holy Spirit (see 1 Timothy 4:7; Romans 6:11-14, 16-19). It is not easy to change sinful habits, thoughts, and tendencies that you have been characterized by for years. A great struggle can be expected at first, but as you persevere with a desire to please God, eventually the old ways will fade and become less dominant in your life, and new ways will become more dominant, and your efforts will be blessed (see James 1:21-25).

Let's Get Specific

Personal transformation will take place in your life when you **identify specifically** what it is that God wants you to change. This is important. If you are general or vague, you will not make much progress. You must have a clear understanding of exactly what should be put off.

So, let's get specific. On the following pages are a list of **Put-Offs** and **Put-Ons** with Scriptures that apply to each.

First, you need to identify any **Put-Offs** that are true of you. Slowly and introspectively, go down the list of put-offs and place a check mark (√) in the space to the left of an area God wants to change.

Second, you must identify the **Put-Ons** that are to replace these sinful habits, thoughts and tendencies. Put-ons are what God wants you to be, do or become. It is very helpful to know what new desires, attitudes, thoughts and actions God calls you to so you are ready when temptation comes.

Finally, with each set of **Put-Off/Put-On,** you will work through the "Personal Transformation Worksheet" at the back of this booklet. The worksheet is a useful tool that will help you implement biblical change into your life. An explanation and an example of how to work through this worksheet provided.

A Word of Encouragement

Do not be overwhelmed if you find that you have many put-offs/put-ons to work on. Concentrate only on one or two at a time. If you are working with a biblical counselor, he/she may single out one or two areas for you to concentrate on for now. Suggestion: If you find that you have much to work on, perhaps you should start with the 'Hindrances to Spiritual Growth' section (numbers 86 - 97). Implementing these put-ons will accelerate your spiritual growth.

As you begin to **Put Off** old sinful habits, thoughts, and tendencies, **Renew** your mind by meditating upon the Scriptures, and **Put On** the biblical replacements, eventually new ways of living will take shape and the old ways will fade and become less and less dominant in your life. You will become **Transformed**. So, my Christian friend, be encouraged!

> And we all, with unveiled face, beholding the glory of the Lord, are being transformed into the same image from one degree of glory to another (2 Corinthians 3:18).

> Now to Him who is able to do far more abundantly than all that we ask or think, according to the power at work within us (Ephesians 3:20).

PUT OFF	PUT ON	SCRIPTURAL INSIGHT
1. Anger/Temperamental	Forgiveness/Self Control/Kindness	Proverbs 14:17, 29, 15:18; 25:28; 29:11; Ephesians 4:31-32
2. Anxiety/Worry	Pray/Trust in God's Sovereignty and Fatherly Care	Matthew 6:25-34; Philippians 4:6-9; 1 Peter 5:7; Psalm 37:5, 25
3. Argumentative/Quarrelsome	Gentle Answer/Peace and Accord	Proverbs 15:1; Matthew 5:9; Romans 12:18; Hebrews 12:14; James 3:17-18
4. Bad Companions/Wrong Friendships	Don't Associate with/Evangelize Unbelievers/Challenge Believers	Proverbs 13:20; 14:7; Proverbs 25:11-12; 27:17; Romans 16:17-18; 1 Corinthians 5:9-11; 15:33; 2 Corinthians 6:14-18; 2 Timothy 3:1-5
5. Bitterness/Resentment	Tender Mercies/Forgiveness	Ephesians 4:31-32; Colossians 3:12-15; Hebrews 12:14-15
6. Blameshifting	Acknowledge Your Own Sin	Genesis 3:12-13; Proverbs 19:3; 21:2; 28:13; 30:12; Matthew 7:1-5; James 1:13-15
7. Boasting/Conceit	Humbleness/Modest Opinion of Self	Proverbs 3:7-8; 25:27; 27:2; Jeremiah 9:23-24; Romans 12:16; James 4:13-17
8. Careless Talk	Edifying Words/Think Before Speaking	Psalm 19:14; Proverbs 12:18; 15:28; Proverbs 21:23; 29:20; Ephesians 4:29; 5:4; Colossians 4:6; James 1:26
9. Cheating/Dishonesty/Deceitful	Honesty/Integrity	Leviticus 19:35-36; Psalm 101:7; Proverbs 11:1; 15:3; 21:6; Amos 8:4-6; Malachi 3:8-10; Matthew 16:26; James 5:1-5
10. Complaining/Whining/Griping	Gratefulness/Praise/Peacefulness	Philippians 2:14-16; 1 Thessalonians 5:18; James 5:9; 1 Peter 4:9; Proverbs 17:22; Psalm 19:14
11. Critical/Faultfinding	Forbearance/Patience/Love	Matthew 7:1-2; Matthew 22:39; Galatians 5:14-15; Ephesians 4:2-3; Colossians 3:12; James 4:11-12

___12. Depression Caused by Bleak Circumstances or Loss	Hope in God	2 Samuel 22:29; Psalm 42:3-11; Isaiah 40:27-31; 2 Corinthians 4:8-9,16-18
___13. Depression Caused by Sin and Guilt	Confession of Sin/Do What is Right Before God	Genesis 4:6-7; Psalm 32:1-5; Psalm 38; Proverbs 28:13
___14. Discontent/Always Wanting More	Content and Grateful for God's Provision	Proverbs 15:16-17; Mark 4:7,18-19; Philippians 4:11-13; 1 Timothy 6:6-8; Hebrews 13:5
___15. Disobedience to God	Obedience/Hear and Do	1 Samuel 12:14-15; 1 Samuel 15:22-25; Proverbs 13:13; Matthew 7:24-27; John 14:15; James 1:22; James 4:17
___16. Disrespect for Church Leaders	Submission/Respect and Honor	Hebrews 13:7,17; 1 Timothy 5:17; 1 Thessalonians 5:12-13; Acts 23:4-5; Exodus 22:28
___17. Disrespect to Civil Authorities	Submission/Respect and Honor	Romans 13:1-7; Titus 3:1-2; 1 Peter 2:13-17
___18. Dissatisfaction in Life/Unfulfilled Desires or Expectations	Satisfaction in Christ	Psalm 23:1; 63:1-5; Proverbs 27:20; Ecclesiastes 1:2-8; 2:1-11; John 6:33-35; 1 Thessalonians 5:18; Hebrews 13:5; James 4:1-3
___19. Divisive/Sowing Discord	Peacemaker/Unity	Psalm 133:1; Proverbs 6:16-19; Matthew 5:9; Ephesians 4:1-3; Hebrews 12:14-15; James 3:17-18; 1 Peter 3:8-12
___20. Doubting God/Wavering Faith	Believing God/Wholehearted Commitment	Genesis 3:1-5; Romans 4:16-21; Ephesians 3:20; Philippians 1:6; 1 Thessalonians 5:24; Hebrews 11 James 1:6-8
___21. Easily Offended or Irritated	Not Easily Provoked	Proverbs 19:11; 16:32; 1 Corinthians 13:5
___22. Envy	Rejoice in Others Successes/ Contemplate God's Goodness Toward You	James 3:14-17; 1 Corinthians 12:26; 13:4; Romans 13:13; Proverbs 14:30; 23:17-18; Psalm 73:2-3

PUT OFF	PUT ON	SCRIPTURAL INSIGHT
___23. Favoritism/Preferential Treatment	Fairness	James 2:1-9; 1 Timothy 5:21; Luke 6:31
___24. Fear of Death	Faith in Christ	Psalm 23:4; 116:15; John 3:16; 11:25-27; 14:1-4; 1 Corinthians 15:51-57; 2 Timothy 1:7-10; Philippians 1:20-21; Hebrews 2:14-15; 1 John 4:15-17
___25. Fear of Displeasing Man/ Manpleaser	Fear of Displeasing God/Please God	Proverbs 29:25; Luke 12:4-5; John 12:42-43; Acts 5:29; Galatians 1:10; 1 Thessalonians 2:4-6; Matthew 10:28-33; 26:69-75
___26. Fear of Life's Uncertainties	Trust in God's Sovereignty/ God's Presence	Joshua 1:9; Psalm 34:4-10; 91:1-6; Proverbs 1:33; 3:5-6, 21-26; Isaiah 26:3; 43:1-2; Matthew 6:33-34; Philippians 4:19
___27. Fears (Irrational)	Sound Mind	2 Timothy 1:7; Philippians 4:13; 1 John 4:4,18; John 14:27
___28. Fearful Over World Events	God's Sovereignty	Psalm 3; Psalm 27:1-3; 41:10-13; 91:1-6; Hebrews 13:5-6
___29. Feelings Oriented	Commandment Oriented	Proverbs 4:23; 25:28; 29:11; 1 Corinthians 10:13; James 1:6-8,14; 4:1-3; 1 Peter 1:13-14; 1 John 2:16-17
___30. Feelings of Inferiority	Know Your Position in Christ	Psalm 139:13-18; Jeremiah 31:3; Romans 5:8; 8:15-18; 1 Corinthians 1:26-31; Ephesians 1:3-14; Philippians 4:13; 1 Peter 1:18-19; 2:9-10; 1 John 3:1
___31. Feelings of Superiority	Glory in God	Jeremiah 9:23-24; 1 Corinthians 1:26-31; 12:21-26; Galatians 3:26-28; 1 Peter 4:11
___32. Gluttony/Overeating	Self Control	Proverbs 23:1-3,19-21; Luke 12:22-23; John 6:26-27; 1 Corinthians 6:12-13; 1 Corinthians 9:24-27; 10:13; Philippians 3:18-19

___33. Gossip/Busybody	Guard Your Mouth/Maintain Confidences	Psalm 141:3; Proverbs 11:13; 21:23; 26:20-23; 1 Thessalonians 4:11; James 1:26; 1 Peter 4:15
___34. Greediness/Coveting	Learn Contentment/Delight in our Riches in Christ	Exodus 20:17; Luke 12:15-21; 1 Timothy 6:6-10; Colossians 3:1-5; Romans 8:5-6; Matthew 6:33
___35. Guilty Conscience	Repentance/Confession	Acts 24:16; Romans 14:22; Hebrews 9:14; 10:22; 1 Peter 3:15-16; 1 John 1:9; Psalm 32:5-6; Proverbs 28:13
___36. Hatred/Animosity	Love, Pray for, and Do Good to an Enemy	Proverbs 10:12,18; Matthew 5:43-46; Luke 6:27-28, 32-33; 1 John 2:9-11
___37. Homosexuality	God's Design for Marriage	Genesis 1:27; 2:18-23; Leviticus 18:22; 20:13; Matthew 19:4; Romans 1:24-32; 1 Corinthians 6:9-11
___38. Hopelessness/Self Pity	Hope in God/Faith	Psalm 42:1-11; 146:5; Romans 15:4,13; 1 Corinthians 10:13; 2 Corinthians 9:8; Ephesians 3:20; Hebrews 6:11-20; 1 Peter 1:3,13
___39. Hypocrisy	Transparency/Sincere Faith	Matthew 6:1-6; 15:7-9; Luke 11:39-40; 1 John 1:6-9
___40. Impatience	Patience/Perseverance/Love	Galatians 5:22-23; James 1:2-4; 5:7-11; 1 Peter 2:19-23
___41. Impulsive/Hasty Decisions	Self Control/Thoughtfulness/Prayer	Titus 2:11-12; James 1:5; 1 Peter 1:13-15; 2 Peter 1:5-6; Proverbs 18:13, 15; 25:28; 29:11, 20; Genesis 3:6-7
___42. Insensitive for the Less Fortunate	Compassion	1 John 3:17; 1 Peter 3:8; Matthew 14:14; 15:32; Matthew 20:29-34; Isaiah 58:6-12
___43. Judging Others	Judge Self/Search My Own Heart	Matthew 7:1-5; Luke 6:37; John 7:24; 8:7-11; Romans 14:10-13; James 4:11-12

PUT OFF	PUT ON	SCRIPTURAL INSIGHT
___44. Lack of Inner Peace	Peace with God	Isaiah 26:3; 57:21; Matthew 11:28-30; John 14:27; Romans 5:1; 8:6; Philippians 4:6-7
___45. Lack of Joy	Rejoice in the Lord	Psalm 16:8-9; Romans 12:12; Galatians 5:22-23; Philippians 4:4; 1 Thessalonians 5:16
___46. Lazy/Slothful	Work/Diligence	Proverbs 6:6-11; 10:4-5; 13:4; Proverbs 14:23; 18:9; 24:30-34; 31:10-31; 2 Thessalonians 3:7-12; 1 Timothy 5:8
___47. Love of Money	Contentment/Pursue Godliness	Matthew 6:21, 24, 33; Luke 16:11-15; 1 Timothy 6:6-11, 17-19; 2 Timothy 3:1-2
___48. Lying	Speak Truth/Guard Your Mouth	Exodus 20:16; Psalm 141:3; Proverbs 6:16-19; 12:22; Ephesians 4:25; Colossians 3:9-10
___49. Masturbation	Sanctification	Matthew 5:27-28; 1 Corinthians 6:12,18-20; Galatians 5:16-18; Colossians 3:5-6; 1 Thessalonians 4:3-5; 2 Timothy 2:22
___50. Overly Opinionated/Overly Talkative	Be Slow to Speak/Be Quick to Listen	Proverbs 10:19; 17:27-28; 18:2,13; Ecclesiastes 5:3; James 1:19
___51. Pornography/Sexual Lust	Guard Your Heart	Psalm 101:3-4; 119:9; Proverbs 4:23-27; 6:23-29; Matthew 5:27-28; 15:19; Galatians 5:16-18; Colossians 3:5-7; 2 Timothy 2:22
___52. Pride/Arrogance/Self Importance	Humility	Proverbs 8:13; 11:2; 13:10; 16:5,18-19; Proverbs 18:12; 21:4; 29:23; Luke 14:11; James 4:6
___53. Profanity/Dirty Stories and Jokes	Edifying Words/Wholesome Words	Exodus 20:7; Psalm 19:14; 141:3; Proverbs 4:24; 15:4; Ephesians 4:29; 5:3-4; 1 Timothy 4:12; James 1:21,26

___54. Rebelliousness	Obedience/Lordship of Christ	Hebrews 3:7-19; Proverbs 17:11; 1 Samuel 15:22-25; Daniel 9:5-19; Joshua 24:14-15
___55. Seeking Praise and Recognition from Man	Serve for God's Glory	Matthew 23:5-7; John 12:42-43; Ephesians 6:5-8; Colossians 3:17, 22-24
___56. Self Centeredness/Self-Absorbed	Consider Others/Serve Others	Philippians 2:3-5; 1 Corinthians 10:24; Romans 15:2-3; Matthew 20:26-28
___57. Self Righteousness	God's Righteousness/Humbleness	Luke 18:9-14; Romans 10:1-4; Philippians 3:3-9; Isaiah 64:6; Proverbs 30:12; Deuteronomy 9:4-6
___58. Self Sufficient/Trying to make life work in my own power	God's Power/Dependence on God	2 Corinthians 3:5; 4:7; James 4:3-16; John 15:4-5; Luke 12:16-21; Daniel 4:29-37
___59. Sexual Immorality (Premarital, Extra Marital, Incest)	Moral Purity	1 Corinthians 5:1-5; 6:9, 13-20; 10:8; Ephesians 5:3; 1 Thessalonians 4:3-7; Leviticus 18:1-30
___60. Stealing/Theft	Work	Exodus 20:15; Proverbs 28:24; Malachi 3:8-10; Romans 13:9; Ephesians 4:28; 1 Peter 4:15
___61. Uncontrolled Thoughts	Controlled Thoughts	Mark 7:21-23; Romans 12:2; 2 Corinthians 10:4-5; Philippians 4:8
___62. Undependable/Unreliable	Trustworthy/Responsible	Matthew 5:37; Luke 12:41-47; Romans 12:11; 1 Corinthians 4:2; Psalm 15
___63. Undisciplined/Lack of Self Control	Self Control	Proverbs 25:28; Galatians 5:22-23; Titus 2:11-12; 2 Peter 1:5-6
___64. Unforgiving Spirit	Forgiving Spirit	Matthew 6:14-15; Matthew 18:21-35; Luke 17:3-4; Ephesians 4:31-32
___65. Unloving	Sincere Love/Serve Others/ Honor Others above Self	Romans 12:9-10; Philippians 2:3-5; 1 John 3:16-18; 1 John 4:7-10, 20-21; Matthew 25:34-40
___66. Unthankful/Ungrateful	Thankfulness/Financial Giving	Psalm 92:1-2; Romans 1:21; Ephesians 5:20; 1 Thessalonians 5:18; 2 Corinthians 9:10-15

Worldly-Mindedness

PUT OFF	PUT ON	SCRIPTURAL INSIGHT
67. Unjust Employer	Fairness	Colossians 4:1; Ephesians 6:9; James 5:4-5; Leviticus 19:13; Deuteronomy 24:14-15
68. Unworthy Employee	Work as Unto the Lord	Ephesians 6:5-8; Colossians 3:22-25; 1 Timothy 6:1-2; Titus 2:9-10; 1 Peter 2:18
69. Vindictive/Revengeful	Pray for and Bless Your Enemy	Proverbs 20:22; 24:29; Matthew 5:43-48; Romans 12:14, 17-21; 1 Thessalonians 5:15
70. Carnal Amusements and Entertainments (e.g. Base Movies and TV Programs, Night Clubs, Singles Bars, Secular Rock Concerts, Casinos, etc.)	Please God/Godly Witness	Romans 8:5-8, 12-13; Romans 12:1-2; 13:13-14; 2 Corinthians 6:14-7:1; Galatians 6:7-8; Philippians 3:18-19; Colossians 1:10; Hebrews 2:1-3; 10:26-31; James 4:4; 1 Peter 2:11-12; 1 John 2:15-17; Matthew 5:13-16; Psalm 1; Proverbs 14:14; 26:11
71. Carousing/Playboy Mentality	Christ Honoring Conduct	1 Peter 2:11-12; 4:2-3; 2 Peter 2:12-15; 1 Corinthians 6:18-20; Romans 13:12-14; Job 31:1; Proverbs, Chapters 2 and 7; 5:1-14; Proverbs 7; Proverbs 10:23; 21:17
72. Easily Influenced to Sin/Peer Pressure	Steadfastness/Armor of God	Proverbs 1:10; Daniel 1:8; Galatians 5:1; Ephesians 4:14, 6:10-18; Hebrews 4:14-16; 10:23; James 1:8; 4:17; 1 Corinthians 15:58; 1 Corinthians 10:13
73. Envious of Prosperity of the Ungodly	Uprightness/Eternal Values	Psalm 73:2-3; Proverbs 3:31-35; 10:2-3, 25; 11:3-8, 21; Proverbs 23:17-18; 24:1-2, 19-20

___74. Fame Seeker/Status Seeker	Lowliness of Mind/Servants Heart	Mark 10:35-45; Luke 14:7-14; Philippians 2:3-8; 3:4-9
___75. Gambling	Faithful Steward	Proverbs 12:11; 23:4-5; 28:19-20; 1 Timothy 6:9-10; 1 Thessalonians 5:22; Philippians 3:18-19; Ephesians 5:3; Luke 16:1-2
___76. Hollywood Idols/Rock Idols	Worship God Only	Ezekiel 14:2-6; Isaiah 42:8; Acts 14:8-15; 1 Corinthians 12:2; 1 John 5:21; Revelation 21:8; 22:8-9
___77. Immodesty/Sensuous Dress Styles	Modesty	Proverbs 7:10; 11:22; 1 Timothy 2:9-10; 1 Thessalonians 4:4-7; 1 Corinthians 6:19-20; 1 Corinthians 8:9; Romans 14:12-13, 21; 12:1-2
___78. Intoxicating Drink/Drug Abuse	Be Filled with the Spirit/God's Temple	1 Peter 4:3; Ephesians 5:15-18; 1 Corinthians 3:16-17; 5:11; 6:9-11; 8:9; Romans 14:12-13, 21; 13:13-14; Proverbs 20:1; 21:17; 23:19-21, 29-35 Isaiah 28:1-4, 7-8
___79. Materialistic	Delight in our Riches in Christ/ Be Rich Toward God	Psalm 73:2-3; Exodus 20:3; Matthew 6:19-24, 33; Mark 10:17-31; Luke 12:13-21
___80. Music Dishonoring to God	God Honoring Music	Isaiah 5:12; Ephesians 5:19; Colossians 3:16; Revelation 18:21-24; Amos 5:23-24; 6:3-7
___81. Pleasure Seeker/Hedonism	Enjoy the Pleasures of God	1 John 2:15-17; James 4:1-3; Hebrews 11:24-26; Titus 3:3; 2 Timothy 3:4; 1 Timothy 5:6; Philippians 2:13; Luke 8:14; Ecclesiastes 2:1-11; Proverbs 21:17; Psalm 16:11; 36:8; 84:1-12
___82. Sensual Dancing	Glorify God with Your Body	Romans 14:12-13, 21; 1 Corinthians 6:20; 8:9; 1 Thessalonians 5:22

PUT OFF	PUT ON	SCRIPTURAL INSIGHT
___83. Smoking	God's Temple	Romans 6:19; 1 Corinthians 3:16-17; 6:19-20; 2 Peter 2:19
___84. Unequally Yoked (Dating, Courting, or Marrying an unbeliever)	Equally Yoked (Dating, Courting, or Marrying a Growing Believer)	2 Corinthians 6:14-16; 1 Corinthians 7:39; Amos 3:3; Joshua 23:11-13; Deuteronomy 7:3-4
___85. Vanity/Overconcern with Physical Appearance	Inner Beauty	1 Peter 3:3-4; 1 Timothy 2:9-10; Luke 16:15; Proverbs 31:30; 1 Samuel 16:7; Isaiah 3:16-23

Hindrances to Spiritual Growth

PUT OFF	PUT ON	SCRIPTURAL INSIGHT
___86. Apathetic Spiritual Life/ Complacent Faith	Diligence/Soul Searching/Zealous Faith	Matthew 22:37; Romans 13:11-14; Ephesians 5:14-17; Colossians 3:23; James 1:22-25; 4:17; Revelation 2:4; 3:15-16; Jeremiah 3:22
___87. Dullness to the Preached Word	Doer of the Word	Deuteronomy 5:1; Proverbs 28:14; Matthew 7:21, 24-27; Hebrews 2:1-3; 3:7-15; Hebrews 5:11-14; 10:26-27; 2 Peter 2:20-22; James 1:22-25; 4:17
___88. Inadequate View of Trials and Pressure	Accept God's Purpose in Trials	2 Corinthians 4:16-18; Hebrews 12:1-3; James 1:2-4; 1 Peter 1:6-7
___89. Inadequate Knowledge of God's Attributes	Correct Knowledge of God's Attributes	Matthew 22:29; Romans 1:20; 2 Peter 3:18; [Jeremiah 31:3; Romans 5:8; 8:35-39] [Isaiah 41:10; Deuteronomy 31:8][Philippians 4:19; Psalm 84:11; 2 Corinthians 9:8] [Ephesians 1:19-20; 3:20] [Matthew 6:8; Hebrews 4:13; Psalm 139:1-4] [Psalm 46:1; Jeremiah 23:24; Psalm 139:7-10] [Psalm 18:30; Psalm 147:5; Romans 11:33; 147:5] [Habakkuk 1:13; Isaiah 6:3; Psalm 99:9]

___90. Lack of Christian Fellowship	Relationships with Growing Christians	Psalm 133; John 13:34-35; Romans 12:10; 15:7; Ephesians 2:19-22; Philippians 1:3-8; Hebrews 10:24-25; 1 Peter 4:9
___91. Neglect of Bible Study	Meditate Daily on God's Word	Joshua 1:8; Psalm 1:1-3; 19:7-11; 119:9-12, 15-16, 105, 130; Matthew 4:4; 2 Timothy 2:15; 3:16-17; Hebrews 4:12; 1 Peter 2:2
___92. No Burden for the Lost	Compassion/Witnessing/Share the Gospel	Psalm 107:2; Psalm 126:5-6; Proverbs 11:30; Ezekiel 3:18-19; Matthew 9:35-38; Mark 8:38; Acts 1:8; Romans 1:16; 10:13-15; 2 Corinthians 5:18-20
___93. No Ministry Involvement	Serve God and Fellow Believers	John 12:26; Romans 12:4-8, 11; 1 Corinthians 15:58; Galatians 5:13; 6:9-10; Ephesians 4:16; 1 Peter 4:10-11
___94. Not Tithing	Regularity in Giving/Faithful Stewardship	Proverbs 3:9-10; 11:24-25; Malachi 3:8-12; Matthew 6:21; 1 Corinthians 16:1-2; 2 Corinthians, Chapters 8 & 9
___95. Prayerlessness	Pray Daily	Psalm 55:17; 66:16-20; Proverbs 3:5-6; Matthew 6:6-13; Luke 18:1; Acts 12:12; Philippians 4:6-7; 1 Thessalonians 5:17; Hebrews 4:14-16; James 1:5-8
___96. Sporadic Church Attendance	Regularity in Sunday Worship	Exodus 20:8-11; 1 Chronicles 16:29; Psalm 84:1-4, 10; Psalm 122:1; Isaiah 58:13-14; Hebrews 10:24-25; Luke 14:16-23
___97. Unconfessed Sin/Unrepentant Heart	Clear Conscience	2 Chronicles 7:14; Psalm 32:1-5; 51:1-19; 139:23-24; Joel 2:12-13; Acts 24:16 Romans 2:4-5; 2 Corinthians 7:9-11; Hebrews 10:22; 1 John 1:9-2:2;

PUT OFF	PUT ON	SCRIPTURAL INSIGHT

Husbands and Fathers

PUT OFF	PUT ON	SCRIPTURAL INSIGHT
___98. Adultery	Faithful to God and Wife/Guard Your Heart	Exodus 20:14; Proverbs 4:23-27; 5:1-23; 6:24-29, 32; Matthew 15:19; 1 Corinthians 6:9-10; 18-20; Hebrews 13:4
___99. Divorce Threats	Forgiveness/Reconciliation	Malachi 2:16; Matthew 5:31-32; 19:3-9; 1 Corinthians 7:10-16; Romans 12:18; Ephesians 4:2-3, 29-32
___100. Harsh Fathering/Overly Strict/ Legalistic	Patient/Nurturing/Loving	Ephesians 6:4; Colossians 3:21; Ephesians 4:29; James 3:17; Hebrews 10:24
___101. Lack of Involvement in Child Training	Instruction/Discipline/Training	Ephesians 6:4; 1 Thessalonians 2:10-12; Hebrews 12:5-11; Deuteronomy 6:5-7; Proverbs 1:8-9; 13:24; 19:18; 22:6, 15; Proverbs 23:13-14; 29:17
___102. Unloving/Harsh/Impatient Husband	Loving/Considerate/Tender	Ephesians 5:25-29, 33; Colossians 3:19; 1 Peter 3:7
___103. Lack of Spiritual Leadership in the Home	Spiritual Leadership	Ephesians 5:23; 1 Corinthians 11:3; Joshua 24:15

Wives and Mothers

PUT OFF	PUT ON	SCRIPTURAL INSIGHT
___104. Adultery	Faithful to God and Husband/Guard Your Heart	Exodus 20:14; Proverbs 4:23-27; 7:6-27; 22:14; Proverbs 30:20; 31:10-12; Matthew 15:19; 1 Corinthians 6:18-20; Hebrews 13:4

___105. Contentious Wife	Peaceful/Harmonious	Proverbs 12:4; 14:1; 19:13; Proverbs 21:9,19; 25:24; 27:15-16; 1 Peter 3:4
___106. Divorce Threats	Forgiveness/Reconciliation	Malachi 2:16; Matthew 5:31-32; 19:3-9; 1 Corinthians 7:10-16; Romans 12:18; Ephesians 4:2-3, 29-32
___107. Neglect of Child Training	Instruction/Discipline/Training	Proverbs 1:8-9; 19:18; 22:6, 15; Proverbs 23:13-14; 29:15, 17; Deuteronomy 6:6-7
___108. Neglect of the Home	Homemaker	Titus 2:4-5; 1 Timothy 5:14; Proverbs 14:1; 31:10-31
___109. Unsubmissive/Disrespectful to Husband	Submissive/Respectful	1 Corinthians 11:3, 8-9; Ephesians 5:22-24, 33; Colossians 3:18; 1 Timothy 2:11-14; 1 Peter 3:1-6; Proverbs 12:4; 19:13; 21:9, 19; Proverbs 25:24

Teens and Young Children

___110. Defiant/Rebellious	Humility/Submissive	Deuteronomy 21:18-21; 1 Samuel 15:23; Proverbs 15:32; 19:26; 29:1; 30:17
___111. Despising Parental Correction	Learn By Correction/Gain Wisdom	Proverbs 3:11-12; 6:20-23; 12:1; Proverbs 13:1; 15:5, 12, 31-32; 22:15; Hebrews 12:5-11
___112. Disobedient	Obey Parents/Please God	Exodus 20:12; Proverbs 1:8-9; Ephesians 6:1-3; Colossians 3:20
___113. Disrespectful	Honor Parents/Please God	Exodus 20:12; 21:15; Deuteronomy 27:16 Psalm 19:14; Proverbs 20:20; 30:17; Ephesians 6:1-3
___114. Foolishness and Folly	Heed Wise Counsel	Proverbs 1:7; 3:35; 10:1; Proverbs 12:15; 14:3; 15:5; 16:20; Proverbs 26:11-12

Quick-Find Alphabetical Index of Topics and Corresponding Scripture References

(Related topics are in parentheses)

But be doers of the word, and not hearers only, deceiving yourselves. For if anyone is a hearer of the word and not a doer, he is like a man who looks intently at his natural face in a mirror. For he looks at himself and goes away and at once forgets what he was like. But the one who looks into the perfect law, the law of liberty, and perseveres, being no hearer who forgets but a doer who acts, he will be blessed in his doing.

James 1:22-25

1. My Problem

A. What problem from the put off list are you working on? This is a particular sin by which you are characterized.

2. Biblical Reference

A. After you have read in your Bible the Scriptures listed for that particular **Put Off/Put On**, choose the verse(s) that best speaks to your problem.

B. Some of the verses relate directly to the subject; others contain broader principles that may be applied.

C. Also, it will be helpful to your spiritual life to commit to memory a verse that speaks to your problem – especially when you are faced with temptation.

3. Insights Gleaned

What are these verses teaching?

A. What observations are you gleaning from these Scriptures?

B. Ask God to make His truths clear to you.

4. Put Off

How have I failed to live by it?

A. Give personal examples of how you have failed to live by the truths of these Scriptures.

B. As you reflect on this, remember that external behavior, actions, and words are easier to recognize than internal sins of the heart. Ask God to expose the root of your problem: e.g., lusts, selfish desires, obsession with a legitimate desire, wrong motives, bad attitudes, unbiblical ways of thinking, etc.

5. Put On

What changes do I need to make?

A. Observe again the specific **Put On** from the list and write it on the worksheet.

B. Remember "The Principle of Replacement." What new way of speaking, behaving, acting, and thinking must I now put into practice through the power of the Holy Spirit? What new desires, motives and attitudes that are pleasing to God must I now cultivate?

C. To help identify heart sins, ask yourself:
- "What thought or desire is occupying my heart that is influencing my words, behavior and emotions?"
- "What am I longing for, craving, expecting?"
- "What is my source of refuge, comfort, pleasure, security?"
- "What do I want that I am not getting? What am I getting that I do not want? How and why am I responding to what I am getting or what I am not getting?"
- "What am I fearing or worrying about?"
- Complete this statement: "If only _____, then I would be happy and fulfilled."

6. My Plan for Change

How will I make these changes? What is my specific plan?

A. When writing your plan for change, it is important for you to be specific. Do not be vague or general. Specifically plan how you will go about making these changes.

My Problem

_____ 2. Anxiety / Worry

Biblical References

Matthew 6:25-34
Philippians 4:6-9

Insights Gleaned

What are these verses teaching?

* God promises to meet all of my physical needs.
* God commands me not to worry about my future.
* God wants me to focus on loving and serving him and He will take care of me.
* I am to pray instead of worry.
* I should not let my mind dwell on things that are not true.
* I must focus my thoughts on what God says is true, then He will give me His peace.

Put Off

How have I failed to live by it?

* When I go to bed at night I am unable to fall asleep. I lie there thinking about our financial situation and how we will make ends meet.
* When I wake up during the night I can't fall back asleep because I start thinking about the cares of the next day. My heart starts to beat fast and I worry that something is physically wrong with me.
* I believe money will bring me peace and security.

Put On

What changes do I need to make?

Pray/Trust in God's Sovereignty and Fatherly Care

* I need to begin trusting that God knows what I need and will provide it.
* Instead of worrying about the needs of my family, I should pray about my concerns.
* I must find my security in God.
* I should be thankful for my husband's job and the way God uses it to provide for our family.

My Plan for Change

How will I make these changes? What is my specific plan?

• I will commit to memory Philippians 4:6-9.
* I will transfer my "worry list" over to my prayer list.
* I will make a list of all the ways that God is providing for my family and all the special ways he has blessed us.
* I will daily thank God for his provisions and for promising to provide for all my needs.
* When I have a hard time falling asleep, I will discipline my mind to dwell on the truths of Philippians 4:6-9. I will pray for God to fill me with His peace and to help me sleep.

> Example:
> • It is <u>true</u> that God has kept my family safe thus far.
> • I will do the <u>right</u> thing, even if it means financial hardship.
> • I will think only <u>pure</u> thoughts about that person who has hurt me.

* I will share with others about the special ways God takes care of me and my family.
* I will review this worksheet often.

Personal Transformation Worksheet

My Problem
What are these verses teaching?

Insights Gleaned

Biblical References

Put Off
How have I failed to live by it?

Put On
What changes do I need to make?

My Plan for Change
How will I make these changes?
What is my specific plan?

My Problem

Biblical References

Insights Gleaned

What are these verses teaching?

Put Off

How have I failed to live by it?

Put On

What changes do I need to make?

My Plan for Change

How will I make these changes?
What is my specific plan?

Personal Transformation Worksheet

My Problem

Biblical References

Insights Gleaned
What are these verses teaching?

Put Off
How have I failed to live by it?

Put On
What changes do I need to make?

My Plan for Change
How will I make these changes?
What is my specific plan?

My Problem

Biblical References

Insights Gleaned

What are these verses teaching?

Put Off

How have I failed to live by it?

Put On

What changes do I need to make?

My Plan for Change

How will I make these changes?
What is my specific plan?

Personal Transformation Worksheet

My Problem

What are these verses teaching?

Insights Gleaned

Biblical References

Put On

What changes do I need to make?

Put Off

How have I failed to live by it?

My Plan for Change

How will I make these changes?
What is my specific plan?

My Problem

Biblical References

Insights Gleaned

What are these verses teaching?

Put Off

How have I failed to live by it?

Put On

What changes do I need to make?

My Plan for Change

How will I make these changes?
What is my specific plan?

Personal Transformation Worksheet

My Problem
What are these verses teaching?

Insights Gleaned

Biblical References

Put Off
How have I failed to live by it?

Put On
What changes do I need to make?

My Plan for Change
How will I make these changes?
What is my specific plan?

My Problem

Biblical References

Insights Gleaned

What are these verses teaching?

Put Off

How have I failed to live by it?

Put On

What changes do I need to make?

My Plan for Change

How will I make these changes?
What is my specific plan?

Personal Transformation Worksheet

My Problem

Insights Gleaned
What are these verses teaching?

Biblical References

Put Off
How have I failed to live by it?

Put On
What changes do I need to make?

My Plan for Change
How will I make these changes?
What is my specific plan?

"Transformed Into His Likeness" is a helpful resource for pastors, church leaders, biblical counselors, small group leaders, and any Christian seeking to lead others along the path of spiritual growth. Several features about this book make it **a handy tool to use for counseling or discipling others.**

The Introductory Teaching, "The Biblical Process of Personal Transformation" stimulates hope that personal change is possible. It is a concise explanation of the progressive nature of sanctification, which will help the person understand how transformation takes place in his daily life. (Sanctification is the process of becoming more and more free from personal sin, and more and more like Christ in our actual lives).

The Put Off/Put On list is very useful for helping fellow believers identify where personal change may be needed. The Put Off list can be used by God to reveal blind spots in the life of stagnant believers and awaken them to spiritual realities. The Put On's are important because a person must not only know what not to do but also what to do.

The Scriptures are a ready reference, pointing to pertinent Bible passages for over 100 common problems with which many Christians struggle. Many of these topics are not found in a Bible concordance.

The Personal Transformation Worksheet follows the transformation process, and therefore is a practical guide to help others apply God's Word to a daily, life-changing reality. The worksheet is designed to involve a person in his own personal growth.

The following is a suggested procedure for using this resource with others:

1. **First Meeting** As a homework assignment, instruct the person(s) you are counseling/discipling to read the introductory teaching, "The Biblical Process of Personal Transformation." It would be beneficial to have him read it twice; doing so will give a good understanding of the process and pattern for personal change that is taught in the Bible.

   During the reading, he is to highlight or underline any statements in the text that are significant to him, and be prepared to <u>explain why</u> he found them to be significant (a significant statement is a direct quotation from the teaching and should reflect what was impressed upon the reader's heart). This will help him to think carefully about what he is reading.

   After the second reading, he is to thoughtfully and soul-searchingly go down the list of Put-Offs and place a check mark next to the areas that "characterize" him (not an occasional problem). However, do not instruct him to work through the Personal Transformation Worksheet at this time. The focus for now is primarily to gain an understanding of the transformation process. This is important because many Christians do not understand how personal transformation takes place in their actual day-to-day lives.

2. **Second Meeting** Ask him to share his significant statements and <u>why</u> he found them to be significant. This will give you a sense of his grasp and comprehension of how personal change takes place in his life. You may perceive it necessary to discuss further some of the key biblical principles from the teaching so he fully understands the transformation process.

   Next, ask for the Put Offs that he has checked, and list them for your reference. From this list, ask him what he would perceive to be his two greatest areas of needed change. Then, as a homework assignment, have him work through the Personal Transformation Worksheet focusing on one or both of these areas using a separate worksheet for each. Show him how to work through the Personal Transformation Worksheet by going over the "How to Work Through… Worksheet" page of instructions, and the "An Example" worksheet below it (on anxiety/worry) as a guide.

3. **Third Meeting** Look over his worksheets. Make sure he has identified his heart sins and make sure his Plan for Change is specific. You may find that you will need to help him develop a concrete and workable Plan of Change, keeping in focus the biblical goal (i.e., the Put On). Then, lovingly and steadfastly, hold him accountable to his plan for change, nurturing him through the transformation process.

4. As you observe progress being made in his life in these areas, ask him to begin to work through other areas of need from his Put Off list.

12 For the word of God is living and active, sharper than any two-edged sword, piercing to the division of soul and of spirit, of joints and of marrow, and discerning the thoughts and intentions of the heart.

Hebrews 4:12